MIXED FEELINGS

LITTLEMORE HOSPITAL – AN ORAL HISTORY PROJECT

by Jocelyn Goddard

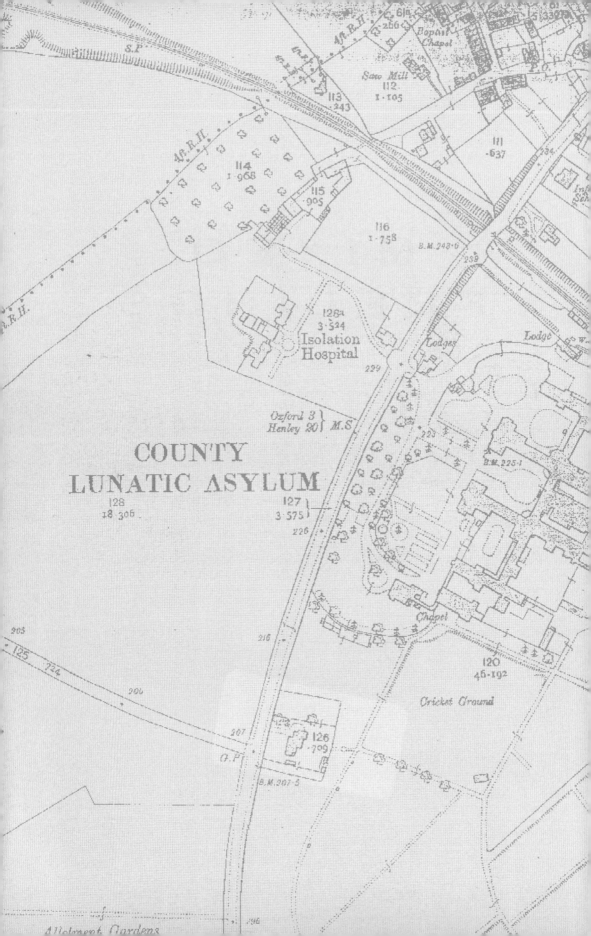

Aerial view 1952

© 1996 Oxfordshire County Council
Published by:
Oxfordshire County Council
Department of Leisure and Arts
Central Library
Westgate
Oxford OX1 1DJ

ISBN 0 906871 25 5

Contemporary photographs by Joan Brasnett

Archive photographs with kind permission from:
J. Bewick, D.Good, D. Hoggins, R. Hounam and
Oxfordshire Photographic Archive

Further information from:
Oxfordshire Photographic Archive,
Centre for Oxfordshire Studies
Central Library
Westgate
Oxford OX1 1DJ

Cover picture: Sports day (Early 1900s)

Preface

This book tells the story of Littlemore Hospital through the eyes of those who received treatment or worked there. It is written at a time when the hospital will have been open for one hundred and fifty years and when plans for its closure in 1997 are well advanced.

The closure of large psychiatric hospitals in the UK is taking place against a tide of concern about whether services in the community are adequate for people with severe mental illness, and about whether the run-down of hospital places has been too rapid and too extensive.

Public concern is further fuelled by adverse publicity following a series of inquiries into suicides and homicides by mentally ill people. There is less public discussion between inquiries and these attempts to learn from disaster, vital as they are, are not themselves adequate to plan a service.

It is worth noting therefore that the closure of Littlemore Hospital is not about the closure of in-patient beds in Oxfordshire. On the other side of the main road, the Littlemore Mental Health Centre has taken shape and now forms an impressive campus, with a range of in-patient wards, outpatient services and an academic centre. The site will be completed as the final wards from Littlemore are replaced and a medium secure unit is added, to allow patients to be treated in secure conditions in hospital, rather than be placed inappropriately in prisons.

The biggest change in the number of people cared for at Littlemore Hospital came not in the 1980s or 1990s but started almost 40 years ago. In 1958 there were 924 in-patients, the highest number ever. Over the next 10 years, numbers virtually halved to 477. This did not attract so much public attention at the time but was not universally approved. One staff member comments: *"Some of them were not happy at leaving the hospital, because the hospital was their home... and I would say that the community was no more willing to accept them when they went out than when they were put into hospital in the first instance."*

The Oxford Group Homes Organisation (set up by the Littlemore Hospital League of Friends) has developed community based accommodation for many people who might otherwise have spent many years needlessly in hospital. Their achievements have been recognised as models of good and innovative practice.

Since then numbers have reduced again. Once Littlemore closes there will be just over 350 in-patient beds for people with mental health problems around the county, including Littlemore, Warneford, Park and Churchill Hospitals, Manzil Way and in Banbury. The numbers are smaller but there is a recognition that in-patient beds will always be essential and there is also a renewed sense of belief in the value of asylum.

The move from the old buildings at Littlemore has mainly been about replacing Victorian wards which were regarded as unsuitable by medical and nursing staff and criticised by the

Mental Health Act Commission. Today the Oxfordshire Mental Healthcare NHS Trust aims to strike a reasonable balance between hospital based and community based care.

Resource centres for elderly patients have been developed at Banbury, Witney, Abingdon and East Oxford, with replacement wards on the Churchill Hospital site. Over the past year day hospitals have opened in Thame with further developments planned in Didcot and North of Oxford. New community mental health team bases have opened in Banbury, Thame, Witney, and Abingdon and will be established in Oxford where three new teams are already in place, and in Bicester.

Services are now increasingly targeted on particular client groups. When Littlemore Hospital opened 150 years ago there was a strong emphasis on social class. Littlemore was an asylum for paupers and, although many had serious mental illness, many others should never have been in hospital and some probably had what we now call learning disability.

There is a shocking bluntness in Littlemore's original name – the Oxfordshire Pauper Lunatic Asylum, especially when set against our attempts to rid our language of stigma.

We like to believe that a building cannot define a service, yet Victorian monuments such as Littlemore symbolise the aims and methods of the asylum movement, and this philosophy seems embodied in stones. The people who built Littlemore suffered no self-doubt about the service or its architectural discipline.

Behind Littlemore's self confident, imposing facade there was also another story. We are given insight into this story through the pages of this book through the eyes of a patient: *"I was wheeled down the corridors. It was like the old buildings of a dungeon. I was wheeled into the old men's ward… I was in with all the old men … I was only a boy"*

We see it through the eyes of a volunteer helper: *"(The patients) would be standing … their arms locked above their heads, just staring into space for ages it seemed before they'd move slowly into another position".*

We see it through the eyes of a occupational therapy student: *"He'd have the patient brought in and he'd demonstrate with the patient in front of you. And there were quite a lot of us there. He'd got this girl and he said 'and your father committed incest with you over the kitchen table, didn't he?' And I was appalled. I was sort of shattered to think that she was stood there in front of us and this was said to her."*

Throughout the history of Littlemore some staff doubted whether so many patients needed to be detained. Dr Thomas Good, who unlocked most wards at Littlemore, continually asked himself why certain patients were not out, but worried about public reaction. *"You could see really how … unless the community was sensitive, it wouldn't cope with it."*

A member of the nursing staff on the female side believed in the 1920 there were plenty of patients who could have gone home, if only someone would provide them with a room. *"There wasn't anything like that for them. Once they'd been in Littlemore Hospital it was a stigma, it was a shame."*

The first sustained attempt to remove the stigma attached to mental ill-health came as early as 1922 after the First World War when the hospital reverted to civilian use as *"a place of treatment" rather than an asylum.*

Every change in regime and treatment brought its own controversy. Unlocking most wards in the 1920s was considered revolutionary and dangerous. When staff came out of uniform it split the consultant staff and for a while two practices continued side by side. The sexual desegregation of the hospital and each new major change in treatment brought fresh argument.

No doubt the mission statements which services adopt as their guiding philosophies today will in time come to seem quaint and peculiar. They are not however new. Today we talk of empowerment, and enabling people to meet their potential; statements of intent are expressed as positives. In the original rule book of the 1840s rights were expressed in negatives - the right not to be abused.

"No attendant or other Person shall attempt to deceive or terrify any Patient, or violate any promise made; nor presume to irritate any Patient by incivility, disrespect, contempt, mockery, mimicry, or sarcasm; nor use of wanton allusions, to any thing ridiculous or degrading in the present appearance or past conduct of the Patient; nor swear, nor address any Patient with a raised voice or in imperious tone; … nor shall they indulge or express vindictive feelings, but … shall forgive all petulance or abuse and treat with equal kindness those who give the most trouble and those who give the least."

The insights from staff and patients in this book reflect the good and the bad sides of the old style asylum. By the end of its working life Littlemore Hospital had changed out of all recognition. Staff aim to keep the best of the old asylum concept of a place where people can feel safe while they receive treatment, while ensuring that the old paternalism and infringement of human rights are never allowed to return.

Advocacy scheme and moves towards user empowerment try to ensure that people who are using services have a voice not only in their own treatment, but also in staff training. Perhaps someone, somewhere is even now writing down or recording what patients and staff think about the new style service. What will those thoughts look like to those who will read them in years to come?

Peter McIntyre,
Michael Orr
Oxfordshire Mental Healthcare NHS Trust

ACKNOWLEDGEMENTS

Acorn Centre, Cowley

E. Allen

P. Baker

J. Bewick

E. Boardman

W. Bowler

Elder Stubbs Gardening Group

M. Franklin

N. Goddard

D. Good

M. Heatley

D. Hoggins

R. Hounam

P. Jackaman

E. Kempson

Littlemore Historical Society

B. Mandelbrote

S. Morris

R. Overall

Oxford Survivors

Oxfordshire Mental Healthcare NHS Trust

Pedlars Sandwich Group

Planned Environment Therapy Trust

J. Russell

J. Soames

Teal Project, Littlemore Hospital

CONTENTS

13   Introduction

15   First impressions

19   Day Shifts, Night Shifts

31   Patients' Work

35   Recreation

47   Fire!

53   Changing Times,
      Changing Treatments

67   Appendix: Littlemore Hospital –
      an Historical Digest

Main entrance, 1920s

Introduction

Oxfordshire Museums, part of Oxfordshire County Council's Department of Leisure and Arts, aim to record changes in contemporary life in Oxfordshire alongside their more traditional role of preserving objects from the past. Photographs and information, as well as objects and artefacts, are collected and archived, as a resource for present and future historical research and interest. The first and most basic method of collecting information about the recent past is to talk to someone who was there and who remembers what it was like. Modern technology has made it easy to record this process of recall, talking about the past, on audio-cassette and this is now called "oral history". At its best oral history can provide completely new information about whole areas of our past which is not recorded in written sources. Oxfordshire Museums collect oral history tapes, which are archived and made available for listening at the Centre for Oxfordshire Studies.

As the time approached for the closure of the main Littlemore Hospital building, once the Oxfordshire Pauper Lunatic Asylum, it seemed that an era was about to end for a community past and present, connected with that place. It was seen to be important that in years to come, when the building is used for another purpose, its outbuildings demolished and grounds adapted or built over, there should be some record left of the changing lives lived within it for 150 years. When the question is asked "What used to go on in there?", some kind of answer should be available. This was the purpose of the Littlemore Hospital Oral History Project.

Only a part of the information and photographs collected by the project could feature in this publication, but all of it is valued and archived by the Centre for Oxfordshire Studies. Additional material is still being collected and would be welcomed. An oral history project is almost always endless; there is always someone else who could tell us something else and reveal another fascinating piece of information stored over the years in that other great archive, the memory of the people who were there. To those who have known Littlemore Hospital over many years, there will immediately appear to be enormous gaps in the account which follows. This is not a comprehensive and definitive history of the hospital, nor did it aim to be. At best perhaps it will make a contribution to a book of that nature, should someone in the future choose to write it. Our aim is to open a small window on the world within the hospital community and allow those of us on the outside to catch a glimpse of life as it went on behind the stone walls and down those long polished corridors.

Corridors (1995)

First impressions

Arriving at a psychiatric hospital for the first time can be a daunting experience.

I was a bit frightened when I first went in there like, you know, I didn't know what it was all about or anything. I'd never had a breakdown or anything like that before... so I was a bit like a fish out of water really.

Feelings of disorientation and alienation can be made worse by the architecture. Buildings designed as a Victorian asylum may appear inappropriate a hundred years later.

It looks like Colditz, doesn't it?

The original design of the building can still have impact in spite of a series of modifications and modernisation.

The beds were in cells, like prison cells, great big doors on them and great concrete, all concrete walls and that. You know, a bomb wouldn't blow it, you know.

Long corridors are a familiar feature of older hospitals.

I was wheeled down the corridors, it was like, if you knew the old films, like, in a castle. The walls hadn't been plastered and painted, it was like the old building of a dungeon, you know, going down the corridors. And I remember I was wheeled into the old men's ward, which was called Windrush. I was in with all the old men. I was only a boy..., I was only a boy.

Institutions such as schools and hospitals are often remembered for their distinctive smells!

The first thing that hit you when you walked in a mental hospital was the smell. It was said that was a combination of paraldehyde, which is a drug, a sedative, which was given to the patients, with a very strong smell, and then paraffin, they used paraffin wax to polish the floors, and then urine, from incontinent patients and it was the smell that really hit you when you walked on the ward.

Memories of Littlemore Hospital in the 1940s and 1950s contrast sharply with Oxford's other psychiatric hospital.

The Warneford was private at the time and I remember that my introduction to the Warneford was quite interesting. I arrived one afternoon to help and there was a bridge party going on - because it was very very select, the Warneford - and it was like going into a large country mansion. And there were these sort of elegant people wandering around and playing bridge, and I carried in the small cucumber sandwiches and such, and got engaged in talk with a tall distinguished looking gentleman who was very interesting. And I came away and the OT said "Do you know who that was you were talking to?" And I said "No, was he a doctor?" "No", she said "He's probably the most mentally ill person in the place! And you'd no idea!" It was quite amusing to me!

The same person remembered her first impressions of Littlemore Hospital:

But Littlemore was a real culture shock - well, I say a culture shock, it was not a culture shock, it was a shock! Because in those days one didn't have so much input from media. I mean the clipped BBC reports were very factual and things that weren't mentioned were...anything to do with sex, or the causes of illness, mental illness, or anything like that. So one was completely naive and innocent, coming to these places and you'd see these people...The state of humanity in those days in a mental hospital seemed pitiful, because the drugs weren't available, weren't known about. And they would be standing...their arms locked above their heads just staring into space for ages it seemed before they'd move slowly into another position...they were really locked in themselves......And they had the padded cell, we were shown a padded cell, there was a girl in the corner, huddled on the ground, it was all sort of softly covered walls. I think they're little... bedrooms now, but they were padded cells then. It was to stop them hurting themselves in their paroxysm of...distress.

"Shock" is a word frequently used by those remembering their first day. Thirty years later the feelings were similar.

Well, I was really shocked. Well, I was very ill and I didn't think much about the place, but after I got better, I thought how terrible it was, you know, because there was a bit of carpet there and you couldn't tell the colour of it because of the cigarette burns. It was filthy and there was cigarette burns on it and you couldn't tell the colour of it, really terrible.

For some it was the condition of the patients which caused the initial anxiety. A retired nurse who started work in the 1920s as "a nice big strapping girl" of seventeen and a half had vivid memories of her first day.

And she brought me up to Littlemore...she used to get every other weekend off so she brought me on the Monday, we come up on the train, and landed me there. I was sat in the mess room, I thought "Oh dear, this is a queer place!" And I looked down and there was the back court where... they were roaming round, the patients were walking round and round, I thought "Oh dear!" Anyway, a lady come by, she said, "Are you the new nurse, from Brackley?" So I said "Yes". She said "Oh, tea will be up in a minute!" So that was good, So we had tea, and then the Matron sent for me. I had an interview with the Matron, and then the Matron's maid took me down to my bedroom. I unpacked and it wasn't till the next morning - I had to stop in bed till the doctor give me a medical, and once I'd had my medical I was to go back upstairs and get my uniform and land on a ward. And I went to the old ladies' ward, A8. I went to A8. And I really enjoyed it. I was very very happy. I'd been there five days, we got two days off in those days, you see, so I went home. "I knew you wouldn't stop!" she said "I don't know what you went for!" I said "I'm not, I'm stopping! I've only come home because I've got my days off!" "You don't like that place, do you?" I said "Yes, it's lovely!"

Littlemore Station, early 1900s

Some people had affectionate memories of Littlemore Hospital starting from day one.

My first impressions were wonderful. I arrived at Littlemore station at the side of the hospital, the porter carried my luggage from the station, helped with my luggage up to the front door... The last day of March I went there and the flowers in the grounds were beautiful so it was a lovely day. And then Matron's maid met me at the front door and took me up to Matron's office and the first Matron...that I knew, Miss MacNicholl was really a wonderful person and I can't remember much just that she said she hoped I was prepared to work hard and so that was it. So then Amy the maid took me down, we used to sleep on the wards when we first came to the hospital, she took me down to what was A3 and the room was very spartan et cetera. Then I was got into uniform somehow or other and then I was taken up to the mess room for tea and I've never known of eggs so hard in all my life as it was to swallow that boiled egg for tea!

For some the settling in process was harder than for others. Most people probably adapted eventually to their new environment and began to join in the life of the hospital, as memories of the first day faded.

And the thing that struck me was, six months after I'd been there, volunteers would come in, and they'd be very shocked by things which I had originally been shocked by and I noticed that I had ceased to notice them. And I thought that was interesting and dangerous. That I'd become part of it.

Farm buildings (1995)

Nurses wore a blue armband to show they had passed their preliminary exam

Day shifts, night shifts

In its hey-day Littlemore Hospital was a large institution intended to be as self-sufficient as possible. Comparisons are often made with a Manor House and its village.

So we were rather like people administering a sort of castle and its feudal tenants in some way, at Littlemore.

It is well known that there was a hospital farm, with pigs, chickens, ducks and vegetable gardens providing food for the hospital kitchens. Teams of gardeners kept the flower beds beautiful and the cricket pitch level. The laundry, stores and workshops provided employment for local people and patients. Many different trades and crafts were represented.

We had a tailor here. They used to come in, I think it was probably a contract with Burton's or someone like that, and the measurements used to get sent to them and they would ready make the suit, but then if there was any alterations required, they used to go to our tailor, a resident tailor who used to be here, a coloured gentleman by the name of Noel Dawson. Here we're talking about the early '60s.

It is usual in such societies that there is a recognised hierarchy, both between the different occupations and staff groups and within them.

The chief male nurse and the deputy chief male nurse, when you approached them you always had to give them a military type of salute. And of course any visitors that came in, you always had to stand. And the charge nurses, they were, you know, a bit aloof. They used to, you know, really shout rather than ask you to do anything.

In the 1920s, female nurses displayed their place in the hierarchy by wearing a blue band on their sleeve to represent the passing of the first hurdle, the preliminary exam.

You'd sit your exam at eighteen months, the first, the preliminary. Then if you passed that you sat your final at the end of three years. And I've got the book there, we took all our learning from..- The handbook for mental nurses. You had to buy that as soon as you got there

- Out of your own wages?

Oh yes, it took us weeks to pay for the blessed thing! Out of eleven and elevenpence ha'penny! Nobody knows - and yet we were happy, you know! Happy as all the birds in the air! Eleven and elevenpence ha'penny wasn't much, I know, but it seemed to satisfy us.

In 1922, when the hospital re-opened after its occupation by the military in World War I, Dr. Good, the Superintendent, made training of nurses a priority. "The total number of the Nursing Staff holding the final certificate of the Medico Psychological Association are [sic] 5

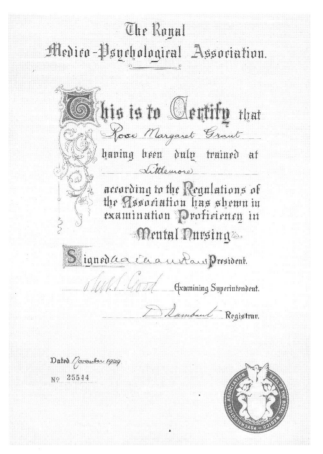

Certificate

Medal worn to show the asylum attendant had passed his nursing certificate

men and 10 females, and the Preliminary 6 men and 22 females. All the Nursing Staff have been informed that they must obtain the Certificate or they will not be retained in the service."

At the same time the nurses' hours of duty were reduced to 66 per week. This did not include the time spent attending the courses of lectures and demonstrations given by the doctors.

In 1948, when occupational therapy was a new profession, students from Dorset House attended lectures at Littlemore Hospital. One disturbing occasion stood out in one former student's memories of that time.

> He'd describe a case, he'd then have the patient brought in and he'd demonstrate with the patient in front of you. And there were quite a lot of us there. He'd got this girl and he said "and your father committed incest with you over the kitchen table, didn't he?" And I was appalled. I was sort of shattered to think that she was stood there in front of us and this was said to her, you know. "What did he do then?" You know, and sort of jollying her along ... I don't know really what her understanding was, it appeared that she was very disadvantaged mentally, but it seemed awfully sad that people were treated like cattle and used to demonstrate... It just rang a nerve in me that I didn't like... the way patients were treated then, they were cases.

During the Second World War occupational therapy at Littlemore Hospital had been a voluntary job, unpaid war work.

> So the Red Cross held this meeting, they specially wanted a librarian and I did some library training with the Red Cross and so they said that.. Littlemore, the military part of Littlemore, Ashhurst needed a librarian, but what they really needed was somebody who would do crafts. And I said well, I would be better at that than at being a librarian, because I had been doing that, I had done arts and crafts for years in London. So I went up there on my own, to begin with. The Red Cross supplied all the stuff, but it was a voluntary job, and it soon became so big, there were so many people wanted something to do and crafts, that I got two friends of mine, one who was an artist friend, who had done, like me, done a long course of art and craft. And she came to help me and then we got another friend who was very good at sewing and things, and also had a car, so she took us up to Ashhurst, because it's quite a long way from North Oxford.... Men used to do mostly their army crests in wool, in tapestry work, and Freda, my artist friend, and myself, we used to go home and set up looms every night - our homework was appalling! - We set up looms for them.... because setting up a loom takes.. anything like an hour and a half, whereas the men could do it in five minutes, to weave it, not quite, but!

The Red Cross provided all the materials and they managed to have plenty of wool and canvas, and the most popular thing was doing their army crests. But we also used to go - we both could draw, you see, we were both artists - and we used to go home every night with requests for what they were going to do on their bits of canvas. We did everything, it was mainly army crests, but we did everything from the Crucifixion to Mickey Mouse!

Head male nurse "Porky" Reynolds, 1930s

Group of nurses and patients, 1920s. Notice the beds in the background, out in the open air.

One task all nurses had to learn to do to a very high standard was the making of beds.

That was the coldest job you could ever have, making beds on a verandah, you know, in the frosty weather. Your fingers used to get numb, you couldn't feel the clothing, you know .... All the sheeting and all that was cold. Because it was all open air, you see, well, there was a glass roof over the top, like.

Young people coming in to nursing in the '20s had a lot to learn.

No, no, I did upset a patient one day, but I didn't dream that I was upsetting him. You've seen berries that form on holly, haven't you? Well I picked, snatched a handful of them off and I was shooting them, you see, like you do, you know with your thumb and finger, and flicking them, like that. I was catching a patient on the back of the neck with some, you see, and he flew off the handle, like, you know, I had a job to calm him down. I mean it was a silly thing for me to do, but I just never thought, you know.

Most of their training was done on the ward. They observed others, took orders from their seniors, and "it just sort of come natural".

There'd be so many come down from each wing, you see, and there'd be a male nurse there for each bath, and you'd be there to supervise and see that he had a bath. You'd probably have to bath him as well, because we used to have what they call, like a dandy brush, I don't know if you've seen them, they had them for horses and that, only those for horses were stiffer, you know, they use them for brushing with, but these were for bathing with, you know, and a large bully beef tin full of soft soap, and you'd get a handful of that and put it on the brush and sort of semi-scrub them over like, you know.

Hydro-therapy baths were also acquired for the re-opening in 1922.

How easy was it to sleep in the day?

Very difficult at times. I had what they call a medical bath... well they weren't for us, really, but I used to have one. It was a tube of - water would come down into a bathroom. Of course the main bathroom for the patients was, you know, about 20 baths in one big room. And you had to be in there to bath each patient, you see. But this one that we had, medical bath, it was .... in the hospital wing. Hot and cold water would flow into one large pipe and be what they call a mixer. And you could adjust the taps and turn that on so that it would come to an even temperature, you see, whatever temperature you wanted. And then that would come in the bath through one tap, you see, and you'd get an overflow which would carry it out the other end. So that water was coming in and going out all the time, keeping at the same temperature. You'd be surprised how that gets you to sleep. That was as good as a sleeping draught, that was.

Oh and we had treatment baths too, that was a prolonged bath, oh dear but it was the nurses who got tired, not the patients, holding the patient in a bath of running water! I find that very nice myself, I used to often lie in the bath with the tap running that was lovely. But no, it was supposed to calm the patient but it wore the nurses out!

An evening bath might sooth an agitated patient, but night times were often disturbed, according to some.

You'd hear them screaming, because they'd be inside rooms near the house, with shutters up at the window. And they'd be screaming and banging on the shutters nearly all night some nights.

The Board of Control in 1929 was impressed by the small amounts of sedative drugs administered. "Another interesting feature is the sparing use of sedatives. At the present time no male patient is having a hypnotic and very few women. During the past month only five special draughts were given for sleeplessness."

Nurses were also proud of their record

Roughly four hundred and ninety certified patients and night after night in the night sister's book they would say no medicines given, no medicines given and not a thing was given and even in the refractory ward you could hear a pin drop, people slept in those days.

Different people remember nights in Littlemore differently. Perhaps they are thinking of different times, or it is the unusual which stays in the memory. A single person shouting and banging at the window might sound very loud in an otherwise quiet Oxfordshire village.
Probably the sparing use of sedative drugs in the '20s and '30s was part of Dr. Good's humanitarian philosophy. His name is famous in the hospital annals, for his open door policy. "Good by name and good by nature" was one comment.

Dr. Good was the one who unlocked all those doors - well, he didn't unlock every door. He left two wards locked. And every other mental hospital was locked, wasn't it? And he was the first to bring in unlocking the doors. And they said "Oh, there will be trouble!". There wasn't any trouble, you see. As long as the nurses were observant, they wouldn't escape. You kept your eye on the door. You'd one door to watch and that's it!

Observation was hard work for nurses.

We had what they called padded rooms there, and you didn't, you weren't allowed to lock a patient in there, you had to be on observation outside the door, unlocked, you weren't allowed to lock a patient in. And I mean that is a terrible monotonous job, for about 10 or 12 hours a day.

Thomas Saxty Good (Superintendent 1906-1936)
"Good by name and good by nature"

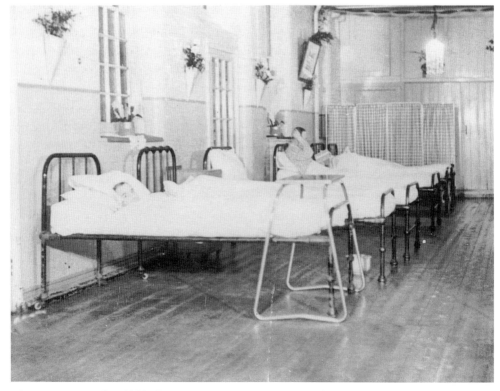

B6 (men's ward) before 1930. The flower arrangements contrast with the spartan furnishings.

Figures for hours of seclusion undergone by a patient were recorded in a special book on the ward and were open to inspection by the Board of Control. During this period little seclusion was reported from the male wards. "The amount of seclusion on the male side was only 30 minutes, and on the female side 61 hours 29 minutes" (Report of Board of Control 13th December 1929)

It has been suggested that this apparent discrepancy is due to nursing staff exploiting a "loophole" in the rules. If a patient was not locked in the padded cell, he was not officially secluded, even though he was effectively prevented from leaving by the nurse stationed outside the door. This practice may not have been followed by the female nurses, who had lower staff-patient ratios and this would go some way also to explaining why there is consistently more seclusion reported on the female wards, although there was also a prevailing belief that women were more unmanageable than men.

Nurses 1928. The sister (back row, middle) is distinguished by her blue dress and the starched bow on her cap. This was apparently very uncomfortable to wear as it rubbed behind the ears and up the neck.

Superintendent's House (1995)

If watching over a single agitated patient in a cell might be boring, it could be a challenge to be responsible for large groups.

> *They (Superintendent) got a big house in the grounds there. In fact, I got into a row over that one day. I was on observation, there was one I missed and he gone round there and he started stripping out on the front lawn of their house! I got hauled over the coals about it. They couldn't do much about it, because I mean, you can't keep your eyes on 20 or 30 at a time!*

> *Edith the cook. She wouldn't come to live with us unless Dr. Good had a fence put round the house to stop the patients coming in. Because we never knew who we was going to find in the drawing room!*

In 1926, a new nurse started work on a ward of elderly ladies, many of whom were "bed-patients".

> *The first thing I did was to get these three old ladies their breakfasts... feed them and everything.... Time we'd done all that, then we had to make their bed, wash them and make their bed and all that - we made the bed, made them comfortable, and then they'd stop there till dinner time, you see. And they'd say "Nurse! When's dinner!" "Oh, not yet, Gran!" "Oh, what we going to have?" "Oh, I don't know yet, can't tell you! You'll have to wait and see!" Then we used to feed them, then in the afternoon we used to remake the beds again... Once a week, they had a bath, you had to take them out of their in a wheelchair into the bathroom, you know, put them in a proper big bath and bath them, and dry them, bring them back to bed again. Then it would be tea-time, you'd feed them, then at night - they didn't have any supper ... then at half-past seven we used to come off.*

A male nurse remembers the routine in the early 1950s.

> *At 7 a.m. you put on a white apron and white jacket and you hung your coat up in the cloakroom. I always remember hanging my coat up because I'm just under six foot tall and I had to go on my toes for to reach the coat. It was said that the charge nurse who put the coat hook up was six foot five! Then you went into the charge nurse's office to collect the clothing cupboard key. The night before, the patients' clothing had been folded and locked away. You gave out the clothing and then went in the bathroom with the patients and helped those who needed assistance with washing and dressing. At 8 a.m. you went to the kitchen to collect the breakfast and this was taken to the ward in metal containers... and breakfast was always a cooked meal and very good, actually. The patients sat four to a table and were served with breakfast. When the meal was finished, all cutlery had to be counted and then a few medications were given out and then the worker patients were given cigarettes or an issue of tobacco.*

> *– Why did you have to count the cutlery?*

> *Because everything which, you know, which [was] regarded as being dangerous was checked and locked away; scissors, knives, forks, this sort of thing, were always checked and locked*

Male staff, probably 1930s. Mr Reynolds is recognisable in the double-breasted jacket. The names of the others are not (yet) recorded.

Former 'airing-court'. Photograph taken in the 1960s.

away. After breakfast there was the washing up, the bed-making and ward-cleaning to be done. There was no domestic staff or porters. And this went on until 10 a.m. and then the order was given for "boots on" and the patients went to the boot-room, took off their slippers and put on their boots. They were then taken out into the garden, which was called the airing-court and there they sat round or walked round, talked to each other and were joined by patients and staff from other wards.

– Were they wearing hospital clothing?

Yes. Each patient was issued with underwear, a shirt and a three-piece suit, trousers, jacket and waistcoat, and braces. And at half-past eleven the shout went out "all in" and everybody went back and put their slippers back on and dinner was served at 12 o'clock. Half the staff went on their lunch break and on return the nurses used to do hairdressing. There was no hairdresser in the hospital. And in the afternoon again it was out on the airing-courts. Tea was at .. half past 4, and again half the staff went to tea. And in the evening they played cards, listened to the radio, there was no television, the first television came into Littlemore convalescent ward in 1952, and then by 1957 all wards had television. At 7 o'clock they were given a cocoa and then started getting ready to go to bed. Their clothing was checked, and any that was stained or required changing, this was all folded and put into bundles, locked away. And then the night staff came on duty at 8 o'clock.

7 o'clock seems very early for an adult to be getting ready to go to bed, even if some would have been tired from the "bumping" and other work, or because of the nature of their illness. Progress, however, was on the way.

Well, television sort of brought it about... before the television started ... in earnest ... at 7 o'clock at night most people used to go to bed.

Patients road-making or re-levelling. Early 1900s. The attendant with the large beard is Mr. Shaddock

Patients' work

In 1906, Thomas Saxty Good, the new Superintendent, wrote in his first report:

> *"The road from front gate to New Buildings, which was very bad after the carting during the building operations, has been remade. The ground in front of New Buildings levelled and drained. Female back Airing Court levelled and partly asphalted. Chapel Airing Court, female side, re-levelled and laid out. The whole of the work on the roads and courts has been executed by patient labour."*

It was normal practice for patient labour to support the economy of the hospital in every possible way, both through building projects and in the day to day running of the institution. Later, when attitudes and treatments were changing, the withdrawal of some of this support caused problems.

"Recent trends in the pattern of treatment at Littlemore Hospital have created a new problem of domestic maintenance, for in former years a large proportion of this work was undertaken by patients. It was carried out by competent members of the hospital's population, many of whom were readily resettled in the community on the introduction of more progressive methods of rehabilitation" (Hospital report 1958-61)

Employment, "keeping busy", was considered by Dr. Good to be an important aid to recovery.

> *I used to have a gang in A5. At 8 o'clock they'd had their breakfast, you'd say "Oh, off to work all of you!" They'd all go and do their various jobs, either in the ward or out of the ward. Some of mine in A5 used to go down to the kitchen and cut up the cabbage... or shell the peas. The patients did all the work, you see. And it did them good, because they'd got something to do. We didn't have any trouble with them.*
>
> *– How many nurses would you have with you for 125 patients?*
>
> *For 125, I only had about 4. Because they were convalescent, they weren't too bad, those patients. But the majority – you come in the ward in the day-time and there would be about 15 or 16 there, all the others would be gone out somewhere, to work, you know, or in the gardens. We used to send some down in the garden for an hour and they used to come back. We'd get the knitting needles – stick a pair of needles in their hands and a bit of wool! We got crafty! Because we did used to cop it if anybody's seen doing nothing. We weren't allowed to let them do nothing. After tea they could do what they liked, but up to tea-time they had to work.*

Patients were recognised to be useful and effective workers within the safety of the hospital environment.

Patients making concrete blocks and teddy bears 1950s/1960s.

I suppose the work-force felt pretty sane and useful. When you talked to them, and thought "why is this person not out?" you would discover that perhaps they were very paranoid, but in a sort of contained fashion. If you avoided one particular topic you didn't bump into the paranoia. And I can remember with those patients thinking "well, couldn't one possibly get them out, couldn't one get them to keep it under their hat a bit?" But you could see really how soon it would come out in the community, that unless the community was sensitive, it wouldn't cope with it.

Perhaps the most well-remembered of jobs done by the patients was the polishing of the long hospital corridors.

They had bumpers.. it's like a heavy block about as big as that seat there [kitchen stool] with a handle in the middle coming up, and that handle was on a hinge so that the head could swing at different angles... and you'd have a gang of patients perhaps 6 patients with 6 of these bumpers and they'd be like this, going up and down the corridor, you see, from side to side. They were wooden blocks, you know... of course those corridors always looked very clean because that was done every day.

In retrospect the monotonous task of keeping the floors shining might seem degrading, but there was a positive side to it.

I suppose to some extent it gave people a certain dignity and feeling of usefulness that say, prisoners, don't have, who are just shut up. Perhaps even though they have a television in their cell they don't feel they perform any function for the whole establishment. And as I say it meant that they did move around, they had legitimate reasons for moving around, and meeting people as they moved around the place.

Occupational therapy allowed patients to undertake more creative projects.

A matron, deputy, she ran the occupational therapy sort of thing and she would have all the old nurses' aprons, sheeting and things like that from the sewing room, all the condemns, and the woollen stockings and things like that, and then these would be used on the wards to make rag rugs, table cloths, tea cosies, all sorts of things like that. They used to, some of them, paint the jam jars, I've got a stool .... and various things like that, and this would be on sale when people came. Visiting days used to be Wednesday, Saturday and Sunday; these would be on sale. And then I think it was the first Thursday in November was always an open day when the general public could come into the hospital. And in the big hall, there used to be all the stuff for sale and obviously the male side there'd be other (things) ... a big sale of work.

Later the sheltered workshops combined handicrafts with work experience e.g. on "the teddy bear line".

The shed that (ten years ago) was the gardening shed, well when I was a boy, I called it the teddy bear shop, because in there we used to have the skins of a child's teddy bear toy. It'd come in like that, and one lady might fill it, another one along'd be stitching it up so much, and then another'd stitch it so much and then another one would put the eyes on it, and then they was all boxed up. What money they got paid for it I don't know. But all the sheltered workshops at the back were doing something like that.

Gardening group working in the village 1970s (?)

33

Originally worker patients were allowed special privileges, extra beer, cigarettes and tobacco. By 1957, patients were being offered "the piece-work rate for the job" for making the soft toy, through an arrangement with a local manufacturer. But payment for work within the hospital was never seen as wages, more like pocket money, or a token of appreciation.

> *They used to make you make the beds, and work in the hairdresser's. You didn't get much money for doing it. I used to get £1.30 for working in the hairdresser's, and in 1974 I used to get £2 for washing up the dishes, polishing the floor on B7 and taking in the consultants' tea and coffee, and washing up afterwards.*

While work for outside agencies brought benefits for the patients in terms of work experience and a worthwhile occupation, there was also a danger that they might feel exploited, accepting lower rates than their fellow workers in the outside community.

> *I worked on Mowlems, that was when they was building the bypass at the back of Littlemore Hospital.... I worked there for about a month, digging trenches, at the hospital. Money wasn't good, all I was getting was £4 a week [a nurse] says "come on" he says "I'm not having you lot exploited" he says "for £4 a week. These other buggers up there" he says .... "are clearing over 17 or 18 quid a week and all you're clearing's about a fiver a week", he says "Oh, I'm not having this!" So he marched us all off and we got paid off and we called it a day. But he wouldn't have us exploited, the nurse, I'll say that. A good bunch of nurses there, they wouldn't have us exploited...*

Nurses and patients could also come to private arrangements. The Sale of Work did not claim all the fine sewing and crochet, for example.

> *Patients were not supposed to work for anyone else in the day time but after five they could do their own thing, so they would quite often crochet lace, it would be snatched to their bosom, and sell it to the nurses. They would do embroidery, they might knit and they would do little things they could sell and get a bit of extra money, because in those days there was no sickness benefit for these people. There were a few who got a half a crown allowance a week, I'm not quite certain whether it was pension or what, but they got half a crown a week.*

It is particularly some of the elderly ladies who are remembered for their traditional skills.

> *Some beautiful sewing. There was an old lady, about 80 something, she made some beautiful nightdresses, all pintucked up the front and flowers-embroidered. It was beautiful. They had what they call a sale of work and sold them... to get funds. It kept them occupied.*

Recreation

In the past, it was considered very important to keep patients occupied. At first their labour was essential to the economy of the institution, but it was also thought to be therapeutic for patients to be at work and out of the wards in the day time as much as possible. For those who were unable to work there were other forms of occupational therapy, encouraged first by nurses and then from the 1940s by trained occupational therapists. In the same way, recreation was recognised as important to the well-being of both patients and staff and activities for their leisure time were planned from the earliest days. The hospital chaplain as part of his duties, held reading classes and distributed books on the ward. In 1871 a field was rented for cricket and football and two new skittle alleys were set up for the patients. In 1902 the grand Recreation Hall was built, in which weekly dances were held with nursing staff, the hospital orchestra, providing the music.

Music and sport continued to be highly valued in mental hospitals and in the 1950s nursing recruits were required to mention any talents they might possess in this direction on their application forms.

> *Littlemore Hospital, Oxford. Asylum attendant required. 5 foot 8 minimum height, ... and then on the application form it had "do you play a musical instrument?" and "are you interested in cricket?". It emphasised cricket.*

These activities were thought to be important for staff morale and to strengthen feelings of team loyalty.

> *There was a mixed hockey team, seven men and four females. There was badminton and table tennis and of course, for the men there was cricket and football. There was seven tennis courts within the hospital grounds. And of course whist drives were the thing of the day then. And the dance hall, the recreation hall was one of the best in Oxfordshire, and there was regular monthly dances. Some of the patients accompanied the cricket team when they went off to play other hospitals, and you went as far as Birmingham in the Midlands and down south as far as Portsmouth.*

There were also patients' cricket teams.

> *They were very good, and they played other hospital teams, and they had a recognised league and everything else and it was a good day out and that... On the way back they used to stop at a pub and have a couple of pints and they knew which pub to stay at. There was one good one at Whitchurch, the Railway Hotel, and they used to look forward to us coming up and some of the regulars used to make a point of getting in early to meet us and that. And the manager there used to put on quite a spread for us. And it was something that was, you know, looked forward to by the patients.*

Hospital orchestra circa 1910, featuring Mr Lusty (double bass), Mr Costar ('cello), Mr Beckett (clarinet) and Mr Truss (trumpet)

Staff football team 1960s

Staff cricket team early 1900s and before 1907, when Mr Walters the younger, standing in the middle of the back row, behind his father, was drowned in an accident.

Staff cricket team, early 1900s. Is it exactly the same team?

Recreation Hall decorated probably with paper flowers, made by patients. Early 1900s, possibly Christmas 1909.

Early 1900s, possibly Christmas 1909.

Patients also looked forward to the weekly dances.

Every Tuesday there was a dance because when the male staff were enlisted they had to either be good at some sport or a musical instrument you see and so they would provide the music for the dances. So there would be a dance from six till seven something like that and of course the men sat one side of the hall and the ladies sat the other. And then I think during the evening there would be one staff dance when staff could dance together. But I mean... obviously men and women danced together but that was how they sat and later on when they changed that and said they could sit anywhere, it was extremely difficult to get anyone to mix at all.

Little had changed since the 1920s, and probably earlier, except that in the early days

We couldn't dance with them. It wasn't allowed... We could get up and dance with the male patients, but... the staff couldn't dance with the staff. Oh no, strict rules!

Segregation of patients into male and female "sides" was standard in mental hospitals until the late 1950s. Segregation of staff was also strictly enforced.

Oh yes, we were separate, ooh we never mixed, no! We weren't even allowed - although I was courting my husband we weren't allowed to walk up the drive together! We weren't allowed to walk up the drive together! I went to the right, and he went to the left, you see. We'd say goodnight at the gate... and if you was caught outside the gate cuddling or anything like that, you wouldn't half cop it! I used to meet him down the road, lower down! Oh, there's always a way!

No, no, there was strict division. Even on entering the hospital drive, you had to walk on your respective sides. And the only time that a male nurse could go across to the female division was if a female patient died, then two male nurses would go there, and collected the body to take it to the mortuary. But before you entered the ward, you had to stand at the end of the ward and get your light key - you had a little key which fitted into the light switches - switch it on and off for to tell the nurse to come and escort you into the ward. The only other time was at Christmas time and they used to allow you to go over there and see the decorations.

Photographs from the early 1900's show the wards decorated for Christmas with paper flowers made by the patients. A traditional Christmas dinner was provided. In the 1920s, it was roast pork.

I remember at Christmas they used to have so many pigs come in, already killed, you know, dressed and that. And they used to be brought in on like a low-loader, little wheels on a truck, you know. They used to bring them in on that, I can remember that as if it was yesterday, seeing these pigs come in, like, you know. Because that was always Christmas dinner, obviously.

Even during World War II

there would always be the fancy ball, fancy dress ball held at Christmas when people really went to town, and dressing the patients up. The food of course was a bit spartan but for these functions the kitchen really went to great lengths to put on a wonderful show for the patients.

Men's ward decorated possibly for Christmas 1909. Notice Mr Shaddock with the large beard.

B1 Ward decorated possibly for Christmas dinner 1909

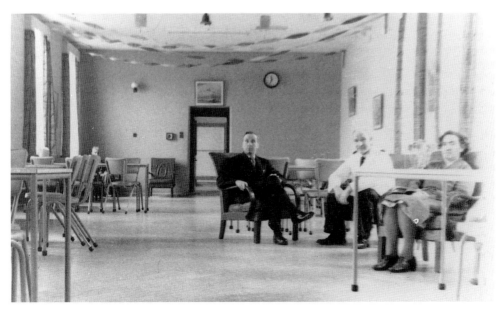

Christmas 1960s style

Early 1900s, probably Sports Day. Nurses seem to be taking it in turns to balance on slow bicycles

Sports Day 1958 Staff and patients enjoying a special occasion

An important occasion for the staff and their families was the annual Open Day.

Oh we used to love going on Open Day .... all the wards were open and it was lovely really because we all used to go, all the mums would take all the children, we all used to go and you'd go to your dad's ward or your mum's ward if she worked there I suppose, and you'd go to your dad's ward and the patients on their ward, I suppose they knew about his children, they were so delighted to see you! They loved it!

In the summer there was another Red Letter Day :

Sports Day was a great day ... the patients had a wonderful time, really. I know they used to have a cricket match on the sports day as well, and there were stalls to have a go on, lovely prizes. I can't remember what the ladies had, I suppose really as Dad was the nurse, we had more to do with the men than the ladies... but the prizes that the men used to get were lovely... shirts all folded up like you get from Marks and Spencers nowadays, and perhaps they'd won a couple of shirts, and they used to say "look at my shirts!" You know, they were so thrilled with the prizes and they were really nice things they used to have for them. It was a wonderful day, their sports day. I don't know whether the patients all had a special tea, but we all had a special tea in the Pavilion.

The children of members of staff were used to visiting the hospital.

And we used to go to the films. It was always a good evening. We used to go in the front gate, we used to turn left, past what were workshops then, and you turned right and got into the corridor to go on down to the hall. And we used to - not when we were little children, because Mum used to take us, but when we got older... 10, 11 perhaps, Mums and Dads would see you off, and you walked round there on your own. It was all pitch dark, you know! We weren't worried at all, we were going to see the film.

Seventy years ago it was all the more important for the hospital community to be offered these different opportunities for recreation, as the staff suffered so many restrictions to their social and family lives, working long hours, anti-social shifts and with few holidays. In the 1920s, three weeks' holiday per year was not considered to be ungenerous.

You got I think it was about three weeks a year then, which was a long time to us, because we'd all been used to one week a year on other jobs, in service, painters, decorators and all that, I mean they only got a week's leave a year, you see. My father's job, they only had a week a year. Signalman on the railway, he used to be on the South Western when I was a kid.

Female nurses, living in hospital accommodation, were expected to keep respectable hours.

All the single nurses had to stay in the hospital and they had to be in by 11 o'clock at night. But if they talked nice to the porter on the gate, he'd come and quietly let them in! Once a week we could put in for a late pass on a Wednesday, if we wanted to go to the theatre. But you had to go to the theatre! You were supposed to go to the theatre! They didn't always go to the theatre - it was a theatre pass you asked for - that many went for the theatre pass, but still that doesn't matter. We got over it that way, you see!

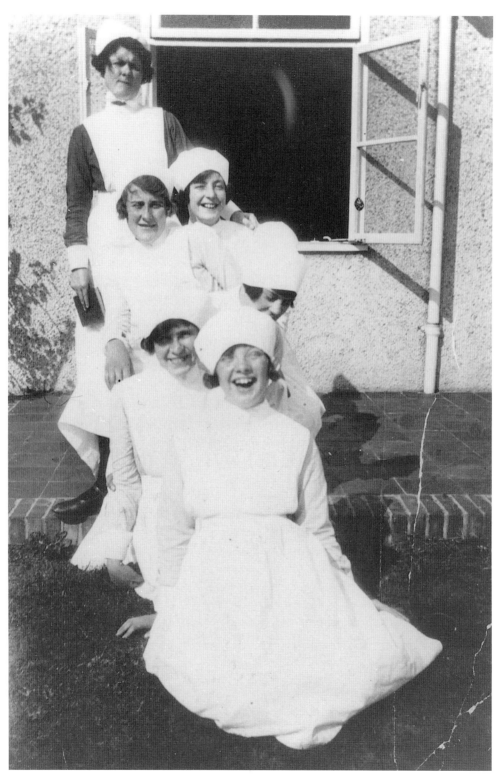

Nurses apparently ready to dance 1920s

They were also restricted by low wages.

> *We didn't have much money, so we couldn't go out very far. We used to get into the recreation [room] in our nurses' home and somebody could play the piano and then we'd dance or sing. You know, we'd spend the evening that way. We weren't allowed to go down to the pub, but down the village a lady, Mrs. Walker, she thought she'd open a coffee shop. And she got a lot of the staff to go down, I didn't, I wasn't one of them, but anyway a lot of the staff used to go down this coffee shop. They had a piano down there and some of the boys from the village went in there, you see, so of course down went the nurses. They'd order coffee and a cake and of course, they couldn't pay for it. so they started running up bills. So a notice went on the notice-board "In future Mrs. Walker's coffee shop is out of bounds to all nurses."*

On their days off, some went home.

> *I was lucky, living near, I could go home when it was my days off. I used to go on a bus, then later years I cycled. From Littlemore Hospital gates to Brackley, about 24 miles.*

By the 1950s, working conditions for staff had improved, but if there were longer holidays, there were still restrictions.

> *Oh yes, very strict routine and that. I knew when I was going to get my holidays and that in eight years' time. I wrote home and said "I have got Christmas off" and it was in 1956! That was 6 years on! But the rota was made out for eight years.*

Nurses outside Nurses' Home 1920s

Hospital showing fire damage to the roof 1895

FIRE!

All institutions dread fire and take steps to prevent it occurring. The risk of fire in Victorian asylums, where wards were kept warm with open fires, and staff and patients lit their pipes and cigarettes from the gas jets, must have been considerable. There was also the difficulty of evacuating safely large numbers of confused and perhaps physically disabled people from the various wards and workshops. In 1847, the Committee of Visitors discussed fire precautions and ordered improvements to be made. Mr. Alderman Carr commented that "The Superintendent should be mindful of the fact that by telegraphing from the very Doors of the Asylum (the Littlemore Railway Station], the Oxford Fire Brigade Engine, and the other Engines of the City and University might speedily be summoned in aid of the local resources." As it happened, the hospital's first major fire, on 15th April 1895, did not bear out the confident assertions of the alderman.

From the Oxford Chronicle and Bucks. and Berks. Gazette on 20th April 1895, an eye witness account:

> Then came the question "Where is the Oxford Brigade?" who, it was stated, had been telegraphed for some half an hour previously. The question was answered by a cyclist, who had just arrived from Oxford and who informed us "they were on the road and would be here presently." Still we waited, until it was deemed expedient to despatch a bicycle to hurry them up, or, in case of a break down on the road, to ride into Oxford. Another half an hour, which seemed much longer to those who were impatiently waiting, passed. The fire during this time was making rapid headway and threatening the whole building with destruction. The clatter of horses' hoofs on the hard road, proceeding at a rate surely not often excelled even by the Oxford Brigade, told of the arrival of the "Victoria".

The cause of the delay was learned later on in the day.

> As soon as the telegram reached Oxford announcing the fire the local firemen were apprised of it. Many of them were quickly at headquarters, and ready to start, but no horses could be obtained to convey the engine. The pressure of holiday times had exhausted the resources of the gentlemen who kindly supplied the horses in case of need. Other stables were besieged, and eventually a couple of horses were brought to the engine-house, but there was then another delay over the harness. To an outsider it seems a somewhat remarkable thing that in a city of the importance of Oxford the Brigade have not horses of their own always ready in case of emergency.

Luckily the resident Asylum Brigade was helped by the Blenheim Brigade, which by a remarkable piece of good fortune had just arrived at Sandford for a competition against the College Servants' Brigade. Eventually they were joined by the Oxford Brigade and the

Abingdon Brigade and the four teams took two hours to get the fire under control. Several firemen sustained injuries, but all the patients, including "several dangerous lunatics" were brought out safely.

The memory of this dramatic event was probably passed down in more than one family.

Years and years ago, when my mum was there, they had a very big fire. A very big fire, I believes Mother and Father hadn't very long been married. I know Mother went down to see if, you know, she could help. People was more friendly in those days, you see. Dr. Sankey was there and of course he was in a way because it was all burning and he said "Oh Goodness!" he said "The night nurses!" He'd just remembered the night nurses, just saved them in time.

In the 1920s and '30s, it was usual for patients to be paid in cigarettes and tobacco for the work they did. Not only were the health risks as yet unrecognised, the Superintendent himself (Thomas Saxty Good 1909-1936) encouraged smoking as "it was good for the nerves." For institutionalised patients cigarettes could assume great importance.

And I was on that to start with, you see, front court exercise, and of course everywhere I went, there was two or three of the inmates following me very close at heel, wherever I turned, they turned, you know. I was beginning to get the wind up a bit! Until I threw the cigarette down, that I was smoking, and of course they all dived for it! When I put that out, they didn't bother about me after that!

Fifty years on, things were similar.

When I was in there I was not well myself but there were a lot of people more worse than I was. I seen people, if you have a fag, they used to come and if you took this fag to smoke a cigarette, they used to come and pick it out of your hand, out of your mouth and things like that.

Nurses also smoked pipes and cigarettes both on and off duty, as can be seen from photographs from the early 1900s onwards.

When a fire on the evening of 29th August 1929 destroyed the female nurses' home, the cause of the outbreak was not discovered. In retrospect the structure seems to have been very vulnerable, being made of "wood, asbestos and stucco on a brick foundation" and the dangers had been foreseen by the hospital authorities who had attempted to ban the use of candles there.

We had to be in by ten o'clock every night, at half-past ten all the lights went out in the nurses' home. And if you were caught - we used to have a candle, you see - if we were caught with a candle we used to cop it! Because of fire, that was, you see. But the lights all went out a half-past ten, from a switch, you know, which went off and that was it!

There were no casualties, but most of the nurses' property was destroyed. although the local papers at the time mentioned that one nurse had lost her holiday savings (£20), and

Patients and staff about 1910. "The Scratch Gang"

At the Nurses' Home window 1930s. Notice the cigarette. When this nurse left to be married, she gave up smoking because she could no longer afford it.

another her trousseau and engagement ring, another of the nurses remembers that some of them at least had so few possessions in their rooms that they made a profit from their share of the insurance payment!

In the late 1920s fire drills were regularly practised.

We had hydrants which were numbered, you see. And if there was a fire alarm, we had to go to the front hallway and there was a row of keys hung up and there was numbers above them. And as you went, so you took the first number and then it followed on, you see. If you was the second one there, you'd take number two, and then you had got to know where number two hydrant was, so that you'd go to number two hydrant, which might have been right round the female side, you see, somewhere...There used to be some rare scenes when we got round to the female side, I can tell you!

Oxford Mail Friday 30th August 1929. Fire at the Nurses' Home.

Littlemore Hospital Fire Brigade 1950s

The hospital Fire Brigade was run by the Head Male Nurse and later by the Fire Officer. Male nurses serving in the Brigade received a small sum annually and extra payments for attending fire calls. The Fire Brigade could be a source of great pride. In the 1950s, the annual fire competition of the Oxfordshire Private Fire Brigades Association was held at Littlemore Hospital on the first Saturday in September. Members of the Brigade were given time off to train and practise for the big day.

In 1964, when the automatic fire detection system was installed and the Oxford Fire Service could be relied on to respond rapidly [without having to send for spare horses!] the hospital fire brigade was no longer necessary.

In spite of the two major outbreaks and several other small fires, there was never any loss of life by fire in Littlemore Hospital. Considering the obvious dangers and difficulties and the very large numbers of patients involved, this is a record which demonstrates the vigilance and prompt actions of the staff and the local community.

Staff after 1895, before 1909. Dr Good stands on the far left, Dr Sankey on the right. Nursing staff are wearing their medals. The style of cap worn by the men, which resembles the uniform of the US Confederate Army, was about to change to a more modern police type. Notice the dog on the lap of one of the sisters.

Changing times, changing treatments

The original rule book of the Littlemore Asylum shows the emphasis on custodial management of patients. An attendant, as they were called, must "count the persons entrusted to him at every meal time and at bed time." If any of his charges were to escape, he could be fined up to £20. He is also required to keep written patient records. There are detailed rules governing the behaviour of attendants towards patients. They were expected to be kind, but firm.

> *Each sub Attendant must keep a "diary" of the number of persons in his charge; the number of them employed, and how employed; the causes why others are not employed; the number of sick persons; the number having fits; the names of the latter class, and the number of fits each has had; also the accidents, or injuries, and refusals to take food, and instances of indecent conduct; and the restraints used, their character, cause, and duration; and of the admissions, removals, discharges, deaths, or escapes which have occurred in his own Ward.*

Staff and patients, early 1900s. Two of the staff, including Mr Shaddock, are wearing new-style caps, while one has yet to change. The two cats are providing some comfort, perhaps. It is unusual to see a black person in Oxfordshire photographs of this age and we can only speculate about how he came to be in the asylum.

He shall count the persons entrusted to him at every meal time and at bed time. And if anyone be absent he shall immediately give information to the Head Attendant. And on the occurrence of any sudden illness, or serious accident, he shall likewise give information.

If any Attendant or Servant in the Asylum shall, through wilful neglect or connivance, permit any Lunatic to escape from the Asylum, or be at large without the proper Order, he shall for every offence forfeit and pay a sum not more than Twenty nor less than Two Pounds.

If any Attendant, Servant, or other Person employed in the Asylum shall in any way abuse, ill-treat, or wilfully neglect any Lunatic, he shall be deemed guilty of a Misdemeanour.

The Patients shall be treated with all forbearance, mildness, and indulgence, compatible with steady and effectual control.

Village, 1920s (?), showing attendant (?) in the street

Ambulances and staff at the "Ashhurst Hospital" during the First World War.

No Attendant or other Person shall attempt to deceive or terrify any Patient, or violate any promise made; nor presume to irritate any Patient by incivility, disrespect, contempt, mockery, mimicry, or sarcasm; nor use wanton allusions to any thing ridiculous or degrading in the present appearance or past conduct of the Patient; nor swear, nor address any Patient with a raised voice or in an imperious tone; nor conduct themselves to any of the Patients in such a manner as to excite envy, jealousy, or ill will among the rest; nor shall they dispute or argue with them, or needlessly contradict them; nor shall they indulge or express vindictive feelings, but considering the Patients as if unable to restrain themselves, shall forgive all petulance or abuse, and treat with equal kindness those who give the most trouble and those who give the least.

The Attendant shall not unnecessarily converse with the non-convalescent Patients, and shall speak principally in reply only, and shall especially avoid the subject of the Patient's delusion - They shall not incautiously speak of any Patients in their presence, nor on the subject of Insanity, nor unnecessarily do any act, the remembrance of which might be hurtful to any Patient's feelings on returning to convalescence.

When Dr. Sankey retired in 1906, aged 75, he had worked at Littlemore Asylum for 52 years and had been Superintendent for 38. (It was suggested that the new Superintendent, Dr. Good should retire at 65.) This would be a time of change after a long period of stability. A new Clerk to the Asylum was appointed and the New Buildings, begun in 1902, had just

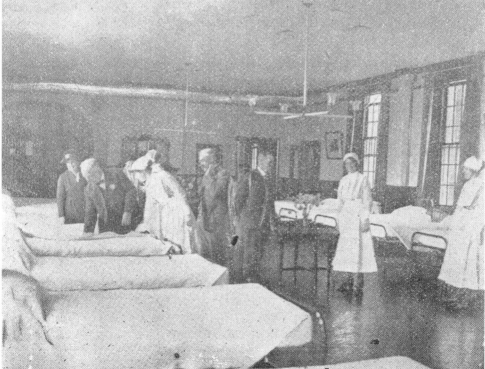

Photographs from the Oxford Journal Illustrated, Wednesday 20th September 1922.

been completed. In 1908 the Board of Control noted "many signs of progressive improvement under Mr. Good's superintendence."

The First World War made conditions very difficult. Nearly 50% of the attendants left to join the army and at the same time an extra 105 male patients were transferred from Rubery Hill Asylum, Birmingham, when it was taken over by the military for wounded soldiers. The majority of these extra patients had to be accommodated in the Recreation Hall.

In 1918, Littlemore Asylum was taken over by the War Office and was renamed the Ashhurst Military Hospital. It was its use for "Shellshock and Neurasthenic Patients" which changed Littlemore from an asylum into a hospital. "It was realised ... the word "Asylum" and with it any idea of insanity ... would have to be eliminated. A thorough re-organisation had to be undertaken:

1. All articles with the Asylum Stamp upon them were collected.
2. All locks were altered and the windows made to open.
3. Certain Hutments were erected"

A system of central heating was also installed at this time.

In 1922, when the hospital was evacuated by the military, it was decided to "attempt to do away with the idea in the mind of the public that a stigma is attached to patients who have suffered from mental disorders and because of their disorder, been admitted to a Mental Hospital. To emphasise this the name of the Hospital was altered to Littlemore Hospital..."

The Hospital re-opened with an almost entirely new nursing staff, and with new departments appropriate to its new status as a hospital, a place of treatment rather than an asylum : hydrotherapy baths, an operating theatre, dental room and pathology department.

The Oxford Times on September 22nd, 1922 was pleased to report that once again "Oxford is leading the way in reform work" when it reported on the Opening Day during which "The public has been wisely allowed to see for itself that the old mechanical forms of restraint have gone, and that men and women are to live in a well-cared for hospital instead of finding themselves plunged into the mad-house of less enlightened days."

During the time that the hospital had been under military occupation, Dr. Good had been able to try very forward-looking methods, including unlocking all the wards.

Psychotic cases were treated, when at all severe, in a special block, the doors of which were open, as in all other wards. It was our experience that the men, as a general rule, were more orderly and amenable, especially at night, if nursed by women. Wards nursed by male orderlies did not, as a general rule, have the same atmosphere as those nursed by women. Then, again, the women had a double training, and the effect was better than with either psychological or general training alone, although, as far as we could judge, the psychologically trained had more control than the ordinary trained hospital nurses. In this connection our observation also led us to conclude that there are only certain men and women who are really capable of understanding or dealing with neurotic and psychotic patients. (Dr. T.S. Good, History and Progress of Littlemore Hospital 1930.)

When the hospital reopened in 1922, only 4 wards were locked. By 1930, "Only 18% of men and 19% of women are ever under lock and key." Dr. Good is remembered for this "open-door policy" and also for his interest in psychotherapy and analysis. He suggested that psychotherapy "is a method which not only assists, but is perhaps essential in the treatment of mental illness."

I got on well with Dr. Good, yes, yes. He'd psychoanalyse you as you went round! He used to say to me. "You've got an awful inferiority complex, Sister!" "Oh" I said "Have I?" He said "You think you can't do it and you can, you know, you just think you can't do things."

Dr. Good also set up the first psychiatric out-patient clinic, at the Radcliffe Infirmary, and while this was no doubt in response to the need to offer something to Oxfordshire patients while the hospital was full of soldiers, it led to his belief that "as a rule, where no marked organic disability was present, cases did better as out-patients than as in-patients." At the same time that the Superintendent was making such radical statements, on the wards, custodial care and attitudes continued and public prejudice proved difficult to change.

Well, in my ward, A5, there was a lot of patients that could have gone home, but the people wouldn't have them. Just because they'd been in a mental hospital, that was it. There were dozens in my ward that could have gone home.

I don't know about the male side, but on my side there was plenty could have gone home, but you see they wouldn't have them. Their relatives would not have them. Once they'd been in there it frightened them. It was sad, there were several of them could have gone home if only somebody'd take - you see, now, you see, they provide them with a room, don't they? You see, a lot of them could have done that, in my time, if there'd been something like that, but there wasn't anything like that for them. Once they'd been in Littlemore Hospital it was a stigma. It was a shame.

Dr. Good took the opposite view of this situation, writing in his report for 1933:

The increase in senile and pre-senile cases may also be accounted for by the fact that the public are losing their prejudice against the Mental Hospital, hence there is a greater tendency to send the old and infirm here to be looked after...

However, he agreed that these old people might be more appropriately cared for elsewhere "in ordinary Public Assistance Institutions if they had better accommodation."

Before the Second World War, in order to manage and care for large numbers of patients without the benefits of modern drug treatments, the hospital resorted to methods of control which would not now be considered acceptable as well as the use of padded cells.

On what was called the Refractory Ward, for instance, patients there wore locked boots, they wore black leather boots with a lock - this was really to stop them taking the boots off, I mean it's not quite as awful as it really sounds. And some of them who would rip their clothes up wore canvas dresses and this again would be fastened with a little padlock at the back and this again was to stop them stripping themselves off. So I mean a lot of things would seem awful, there was in fact some reason for it.

From 1936, there was another new Superintendent, Dr. Armstrong, and as war broke out, new treatments were being introduced to the hospital; malaria therapy, insulin coma and shock therapy. The convulsive drugs Cardiazol and Triazol were replaced by electro-convulsive therapy [ECT] in 1941, perhaps because these drugs were no longer able to be imported. Treatments which at first seemed "somewhat heroic" to Dr. Armstrong were now thought "of most value in hastening remission or recovery not only in schizophrenic conditions but in states of excitement or depression." (Superintendent's report for 1941).

And the methods of treatment were fairly primitive. They were using insulin comas for schizophrenia and we were also using electro-convulsive therapy without the anaesthetics and the muscle relaxants that they now have. So that was a fairly bizarre and horrific sort of treatment. It did have the effect of making people more available, people who had been completely shut off in depression and who perhaps were not moving and not eating and not defecating. They did become more accessible to other forms of treatment with the shocks. They seemed to sort of break up the pattern in the brain in what could be a constructive fashion.

– So it was still a fairly new treatment, then?

Yes, yes. It had been noticed that people with schizophrenia didn't have epilepsy; and on that inadequate basis they thought they would try electro-convulsive therapy for them. But it didn't do very much for schizophrenia, but it did help people with depression. And it came in on that quite inadequate basis. I never had to do anything with the insulin comas, thank goodness, which looked to me a very scary kind of business.

ECT has remained a controversial treatment, which in spite of its gentler application, with muscle relaxants and sedatives, and its benefits to some patients, can still cause feelings of great anxiety.

I've known some people waiting to have it [ECT] and screamed out, you know, at the last minute they didn't want to have it.

ECT is a funny thing, because you can come out of it as if you'd been in a sleep, another time you can come out of it as if you'd been on the drink, like having a hangover and sometimes, I don't know if you've ever worn a hat and you've hung it up. And sometimes you feel it's still on your head, sometimes you could feel something like that as if you were still wearing a hat or something.

The desire to find physiological causes and cures for mental illness led to other "somewhat heroic" treatments.

There was one thing they were doing then... it was quite a new thing... this was an operation... where they would put a knife in through the skull and would sever the connections between one part of the brain and the other. Leucotomy. We had a pre-leucotomy and a post-leucotomy patient and we were able to sort of assess. And the post one was just like a sheep and you could see that it took all their volition, all their will, all their motivation, robbed them of a quality of life completely. They were docile, amenable, easy to manage but they had no quality of life. And of course this is why they stopped it. But... it did I suppose to them appear to be progress because these people were completely over the top, they were unmanageable, and so something had to be done, they thought, and that would be the answer, but it wasn't the answer. So they stopped it.

Within their context and at that time, methods and treatments which now seem inhumane and bizarre, were accepted as perhaps rather desperate measures taken to relieve an intractable situation.

I didn't question leucotomy at the time, I thought this is a bit extreme, but I didn't question it. I thought Oh well yes, you know. I suppose if I'd worked with it longer, that was just one lecture.

In 1959 came a new Mental Health Act and a new Superintendent, the last to use that title, Dr. Mandelbrote. Again this was a time of great change. In 1958, hospital numbers were at their highest, 924 in-patients. In the next 10 years, the numbers would almost halve, to 477 in 1968-9, the beginning of the downward trend. The number of patients compulsorily detained dropped immediately to about 3%, as Dr. Mandelbrote and his team re-classified patients who had been certified for many years. All wards were now to be unlocked and for the first time in over 100 years, male and female patients would no longer be segregated. Some hospitals carried out this process of de-segregation very gradually. In Littlemore, over 600 patients were moved and reorganised on a single day.

In 1959, I think it is, the 3rd October. And we had been categorising and categorising and categorising patients, you know ever since Dr. Mandelbrote took over. We had been taken to Gloucester to see his hospital you know, to experience all this and of course there was a great deal of worry about, when men and female patients got together what would happen and all sorts of things; but anyhow the 3rd of October, that Saturday, I think it was a Saturday that we did it, we had to move all these patients. And I mean they had been told, and they had been taken to the wards to see them. Obviously many of the patients were very anxious about their lives being upset like this you know... but anyhow we got up as usual in the morning and had breakfast and I came on duty and had breakfast and then came this mammoth task of moving everyone and well... by the end of the day I'd lost an old lady, oh Lord couldn't find her anywhere and oh we searched the grounds, it was an old lady of 80 and a harmless old - anyhow the next morning she was found down in the cricket pavilion fast asleep quite warm and dry, but it was a worrying night I can tell you!

The hospital continued to have two "sides", no longer divided by gender, but by treatment and methods. The two consultant units worked along different lines, with one side following more traditional methods while the other developed the concept of the therapeutic community. 4 wards were combined to form the new Phoenix Unit, with 120 patients. These new ideas were not universally welcomed.

The minute we were appointed, we suffered from then on. A lot of staff had been there a long time, trained there, and there was a lot of strong feeling. Because in about a year and a half

Staff line up on Sports Day 1958

or two years, we started to come out of uniform, and I was called a traitor, and things like
that. And I mean you didn't need uniform. In the winter you perished and in the summer
you were roasting! You'd long blue frocks.. stiff collars, you were like a vicar or something!

New multi-disciplinary teams threatened the old hierarchy.
A lot of them wore uniform almost to the end day ... the old staff that had been there for
years and years. I mean, that was status if you'd a uniform on, everybody knew you were a
sister.

New drugs had helped to allow patients more independence and to participate more fully in
working towards their own recovery.
The thing I liked about Mandelbrote, it was group therapy... Every Tuesday, unless it was
unavoidable and he couldn't make it, all the staff and all the patients met in the big room
upstairs in one big circle. And that was every Tuesday. He came himself and took part in a
whole group... and we found that very good. It could get very hectic at times, you know.

Once again Oxford was leading the way and the '60s were an exciting time. The next big step
towards reducing the number of long-stay patients was the development of the group home
system, with back up by nurses working in the community, outside the hospital. Patients
who had lived so long in the hospital that it had become their home, were now helped
towards living independently again.
They might have been in hospital about forty years. And some of them, of course, were not
happy at leaving the hospital, because the hospital was their home, they had a good social

life there, and I would say generally speaking that the community was no more willing to accept them when they went out than when they were put into hospital in the first instance. As I've said I never asked neighbours whether they minded because I felt that inferred that there was something to mind. I should just smile, "nice day!" and all this and I should have got on with neighbours and we found some neighbours would have nothing to do with them. These people were going out of hospital where they would be absolutely forbidden ever to put a light bulb in if it went out. They were not used to tin openers so [if] they got a tin of soup or a tin of peas they couldn't use those, so they would have to go to a neighbour - that sort of thing. So it was the little things but this is always the same in life, it's the little things rather than the big things. They had been forbidden to touch an electric thing in hospital. Well, some of them went into hospital when there wasn't any electricity... their knowledge of a home was where there was gas and they cooked on a coal fire, possibly.

The community nursing team provided support and supervision.

So we looked after them, I feel we looked after them very well. We did a weekly visit to all of them, you see, and we could listen to their problems and so forth. And if somebody wasn't well he would readmit them to the hospital. This didn't often happen, but if necessary they could be readmitted for a short time... and then they would go back to the home because as far as, certainly, as far as I was concerned and he [Dr. McKnight] was concerned, I would always call them "seven-eighths" homes because I felt this was as far as they were likely to get, but it was quite possible they could go on.

Ley Clinic, 1960s

Ashhurst Clinic, 1960s

Living in a group home is perhaps now a transitional stage for someone recovering from a hospital admission who needs a new home in the community.

> *The doctor thought I might get more of a chance, he says "you're not getting much scope in here... we think it would be a good thing if you went to a group home." It made a lot of sense.*

Living in shared accommodation can bring people close to one another's problems.

> *This will make you laugh, it weren't funny when it happened.. it was the first night I was there, this girl went crazy with a meat axe, and she chopped all the banister up. She asked me for a cigarette, she was all right and then I heard this noise and the police was standing on the stairs and they said quick, run, you know, and I run past the door and she had an axe in her hand! She chopped up a chair and chopped the windows up. They had to break down the door and get her.*

Medication may help to control symptoms, but it can be hard to accept an indefinite need to take it.

> *The thing that makes me annoyed, you've got to take the medication, right? I don't like the injections and the tablets, but I've got to have them, you know. And if I don't take them, I'm not allowed to stay in group homes.*

The move towards independent living and care in the community has meant the end of an era for the large psychiatric institutions. All over the country they are closing. Many are being demolished. Some will not be sorry to see the old hospital close.

It's not the same [now] it's not the same atmosphere.. I'm glad I'm out.. it's lost that togetherness. Where we all pulled together.. I've been lucky, I'm in a group home… and I get on well with the nurses and the staff in there, I wouldn't want to move from there. It's done its job for me, anyhow…it's done me good, I don't know about other people.. I'd like to see it close and people have more say in life.

Other reactions to the closure:

I should think it should stay open really, because there's a lot of people need caring for and they ain't got a place for them, that little place ain't going to hold a lot of people.

Well, mixed [feelings] really, because I met a few nice blokes there, but that one what died, it.. upset me.. and I didn't want to be there.

To tell the truth I really never think of it, I'm just glad I'm out, and that's about it.

I like a lot of old buildings, but I don't think it's right to be a hospital. I think people should be .. where they're not so scared. Something like the new building that's just been open. Where they feel safe and know they can get well and be able to go home again, not somewhere they feel more depressed and more ill and think they're never going to come out. The great big rooms and things are scary, the great big long corridor, reminds you of a prison, you see.

Staircase (1995)

APPENDIX

Littlemore Hospital – Historical Digest

1840– Joseph Henley-Warner, M.P. instigates the establishment of an Oxfordshire **1843** hospital. In the Spring of 1843, 15 acres are purchased at Littlemore for £2,500.

1846 Oxford County Pauper Lunatic Asylum opens its doors on the 1st August. General rules published. Treatment, diet and care of patients based on the current ideals of moral management and non-restraint. The hospital's first Medical Superintendent is William Ley, who remained in charge until 1868.

1847 An additional 6.5 acres purchased for the construction of a new wing.

1848 Total number of patients at the hospital is 234. One dormitory contains 42 beds. The Committee of Visitors report noted the purchase of the Chaplain's house; the addition of a new wing at either end of the original asylum; enlargement of the Chapel, Kitchen and Laundry; the rebuilding of pig sties, and that the hospital was running in an "entirely satisfactory" manner.

1851 Total number of patients is 340.

1853 The report of the Committee of Visitors proposes to introduce "an Industrial System among the mechanical portion of the patients who may be sufficiently convalescent to work at their trades".

1867 Total number of patients is 510. Additional land purchased. The highest salary is that of William Ley, at £450, and the lowest salary that of an indoor kitchen maid at £10.

1868 It is decided to light the hospital with gas.

1870 A wall forming a boundary to the railway is built.

1875 The hospital is visited by Prince Leopold. Extensive construction of fire hydrants undertaken.

1877 The Superintendent's Report states that patients enjoy a weekly Dance, cricket in summer, and theatricals and penny readings in winter.

1879 Copper baths replaced by porcelain.

1882   A burial ground is designated.

1883   A new Chapel is built. Electric fire alarms placed throughout the buildings to complement the well rehearsed Patients' Fire Brigade.

1888   Original capital debt of the hospital is wholly discharged. A local government   Act transfers management of the asylum from the Justices in Quarter Sessions to the County Council.

1893   Maintenance rate for patients' care falls to its lowest recorded amount of 7s6d.

1895   Fire destroys the upper floors of the south wing of the women's side of the asylum.

1898   Having reached 438 internments, the burial ground is enlarged.

1901   An additional 53 acres of land is purchased for gardens and expansion.

1908   Total number of patients is 660. The ratio of patients : staff is 12 : 1. 115 patients are received from Rubery Hill Asylum in Birmingham.

1914   War causes staffing problems, overcrowding, and a drastic reduction in dietary resources, but admissions are low and thought to be so because of the riddance of "unemployment and its consequent evils" making mental disorders "almost non-existent".

1917   150 patient deaths are recorded (the result of cold weather and patient relocation).

1918   The asylum is handed over to the Military Authorities, and all patients are transferred elsewhere.

1922   The asylum is reopened and henceforth known as Littlemore Hospital. The hospital now has electric lighting throughout.

1928   20 cottages for married staff are constructed.

1929   Cinema created. Nurses quarters destroyed by fire.

1931   Total number of patients is 776. Mental Treatment Act provides for voluntary patients and treatment of confused patients without certification.

1934   New sewage system built. X-ray equipment installed.

1935 A sound system is added to the cinema, amid controversy. Nurses' hours are reduced to 54 per week. A large greenhouse is built on the grounds.

1938 A tractor is purchased for hospital use. A hard tennis court is constructed.

1939 First uses of Shock Therapy. Outbreak of war leads to all patients being issued with gas masks. Two wards requisitioned by the Army Medical Service.

1940 Total number of patients is 901. Gate Lodge completed.

1941 Purchase of E.C.T. equipment. The Army Medical Service requisitions two more wards.

1946 Female patient found murdered. NHS Act creates a Regional Health Board. The military section of the hospital is closed.

1956 The Ashhurst Clinic is opened by Viscount Nuffield.

1959 The Mental Health Act is passed. The Phoenix Unit and the Mayo Unit become mixed sex wards.

1966 The League of Friends establishes a house for patients moving out of Littlemore Hospital. The first community psychiatric nurse is appointed from Littlemore Hospital to work with the Donnington Health Clinic.

1969 The Sick Unit is built.

1970 The Ley Clinic opens for the treatment of drug addiction and alcoholism.

1972 A dry-cleaning system and a swimming pool is constructed.

1973 Offices, garages, and a new boiler house are constructed.

1975 NHS reorganisation makes Littlemore Hospital the centre of the Isis Group of Hospitals.

1994 Oxfordshire Mental Healthcare NHS Trust is established.

1996 Littlemore Hospital is 150 years old. Closure is scheduled for 1997. Total number of staff is 1,000, with 98 nurses working in the community. Total number of inpatient beds (in several locations) is 350.

Littlemore Hospital Superintendent Physicians

Dr W Ley	1846–1868
Dr H Sankey	1868–1906
Dr T S Good	1906–1936
Dr R W Armstrong	1936–1959
Dr B Mandelbrote	1959–1974

Reorganisation of the NHS resulted in changes to the organisation structure.

The first General Manager in 1985 was Dr M Orr, who was appointed Chief Executive in 1994.

Aided by a donation from FAMOS,
Friends of Archives Museums and Oxfordshire Studies.